Alpha 3: Thaw Out

Written by Catherine Lenahan

Illustrated by Natalia Gubanova

Paul lived on Alpha 3 with his mum and pet hamster, Jaws.

Alpha 3 was a cold planet. If people went outside, they could freeze.

Alpha 2 looks perfect. Nobody can live on Alpha 1 because of the lightning storms.

I'd like to roll down that mountain just there!

The clouds look full of snow today.

Paul thought his mum was an author.

I enjoyed this new book, Mum!

But she was really a super-villain with a secret plan!

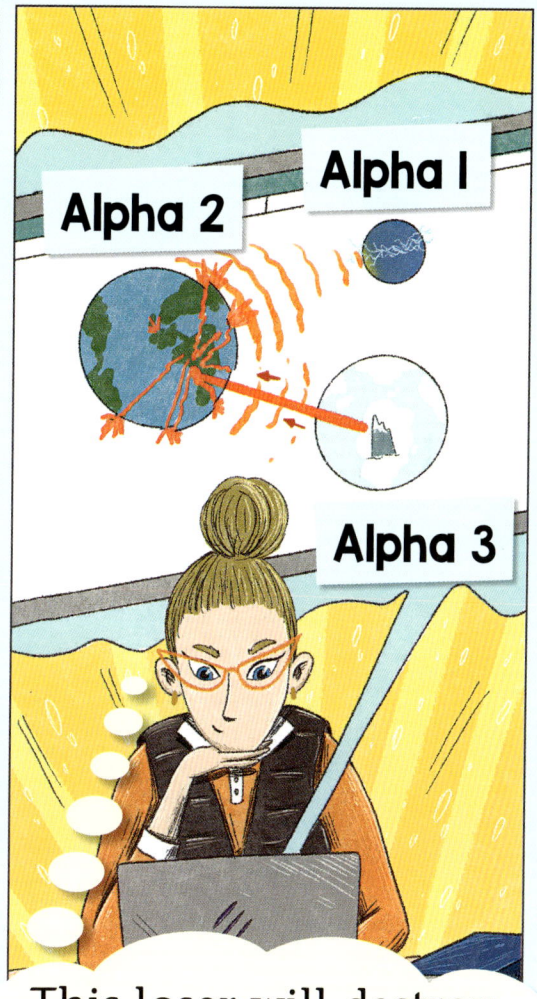

This laser will destroy Alpha 2, but the heat will thaw out Alpha 3.

One day, Paul was running at dawn when he tripped and …

ZAP!

What was that?

His eyes had burned a hole in the track!

Paul kept his new superpower a secret.

"Tell nobody, Jaws!"

Paul soon found ways to control his skills when nobody was around.

"Go, Jaws!"

Paul's teacher saw him one evening …

"Let me help you."

"I'm training children with superpowers."

"That sounds amazing, Mr Proudfoot. Just don't tell my mum!"

Mr Proudfoot took Paul to meet the superpower children.

I'm Scout. I can hear things from far away.

I can make annoying sounds! I'm Volume Boy!

Why is your mum inside a volcano? That's where super-villains hang out in comic books!

She's going to destroy Alpha 2 to collect its heat.

Volume Boy got everyone safely underground.

Paul collected Jaws.

Mr Proudfoot flew them to the volcano.

"She's down there."

"We need to stop Mum."

Paul burned a long tunnel into the side of the volcano.

Nearly there.

Jaws went speeding down the tunnel.

Whoo-hoo!

Paul used his superpower to burn tunnels under the volcano.

This boiling magma will thaw Alpha 3 from below the ground.

Superpower children to the rescue!

Phonics Practice

Say the sound and read the words.

/ur/	ir

bird   shirt   twirl   first   thirsty

/ur/	er

term   herb   stern   person   alert

/ou/	ou

out   about   cloud   scout   found

/oi/	oy

boy   toy   enjoy   royal   destroy

Can you say your own sentences using some of the words on these pages?

What other words do you know that are spelled in these ways?

| /or/ | au |

haul   launch   August   jaunt   author

| /or/ | aw |

saw   paw   raw   claw   yawn   shawl

Common exception words

their   people   Mr   Mrs   looked   called

We may say some words differently because of our accent.

Talk about the story

Answer the questions:

1 Which planet was Paul's mum planning to destroy?

2 How did Scout and Paul get to the volcano?

3 What was Paul's mum's super-villain name?

4 Why was Jaws important in the story?

5 Who would you trust with a big secret?

6 Why do people find it difficult to live in very cold places?

Can you retell the story in your own words?